Victoriana

Other books by Emily Isaacson:

Little Bird's Song

Voetelle

The Fleur-de-lis Vol I-III

The Sunken Garden (limited edition)

Hours From A Convent

Ignatia

House of Rain

Snowflake Princess

A Familiar Shore

City of Roses

Victoriana

Emily Isaacson

The Poetry Book Series
Potter's Press

Cover design and interior layout: Voetelle Art & Design
Cover photo © *Alexandr Vasilyev* X Fotolia.

ISBN: 978-1-329-59208-7

First Edition
First Printing: 2015

The Poetry Book Series

Published by:

 Potter's Press

 A division of the Emily Isaacson Institute
P.O. Box 3366
Mission, B.C. Canada V2V 4J5
www.emilyisaacsoninstitute.com

Dedicated to Princess Charlotte

Weak hand closed round the gold,

Held and displayed it,

Palmed in a monstrance-hold:

In sovereign splendour

New meaning was revealed:

It was not, to her wonder,

Mere poetry she held.

———————— ••••◗◖•••• ————————

Ruth Pitter, End of Drought

Contents:

Victorian Roads / 61

Preface

This small book of poems invites you to discover poetry through the eyes of Emily Isaacson. This collection of her select poetry touches on all that she has claimed as sacred in her life:

> "All that she claimed as sacred in her life,
> are as the artefacts for a future art gallery.
> As a child, she collects the rocks,
> shells and seaweed of the shore for her museum;
> sea stars are the lights of Stella Maria.
> Later, as a gallery attendant, she leads us on a tour
> of the museum of human life, its first conception
> through final breath and beyond."

—*Isaacson, "Door to the Sea"*

Isaacson is a proponent and validator of the value of human life and all that is cherished. She speaks in her poet's voice into all that has meaning in building not only a person but a human race. To understand what it means to be intrinsically human, and also party to the Divine, there is a moment of revelation. In this light of transcendence we are given more than a memento or souvenir, we are given a symbol and a sign.

The signs of life guide our way as we travel life's road. The roadmap is one we can comprehend, and navigate from. Our compass may include many works of literature, and the observation of others. Isaacson has said that the open page is like the open road. There is the freedom of independence. The maternity of dark's womb becoming brightness, a descant into dawn.

Victoriana lets us in on stirring recollections of the soul. These writings reflect both the inner and outer voice of dialogue, and this is what draws a reader into the story or word picture. Dialogue is first and foremost an invitation; it allows one speaker to describe to another their inner turmoil, crisis, and hostility. Yet it also allows for resolution, when the speakers work together with inclusive language to resolve the conflict.

Isaacson delineates through characterization and the process of dialogue the healing of the human soul. Dialogue helps us to understand our use of language and the language of others in rectifying any imbalance in our internal and external world. There are both internal and external voices. The language of conflict and its resolution allow us to see through a window into the soul, and map its terrain. Our view of the inner landscape widens, and we can see the domain.

Domains of the heart are closely guarded by words. Words are like the key which unlock the door to our intellect, understanding and wisdom. Using appropriate words to demonstrate our inner landscape help us more accurately communicate, and more adeptly write. Creative writing is concerned with both a character's inner world and outer one. Learning about creative communication helps us be writers who consider all the angles to existence, as does Isaacson.

The deities of verse converge in *Victoriana*, this time, not as witches, as in the opening of Macbeth, but the trinity in open anthem to a new Isaacson in black and white. Unlike her past, Isaacson is stymied and didactic, her romance is bold, her wherewithal unabated, and her exacting end within sight. Isaacson will again show a proud and vivid front to the army that is relentless in its patriotism.

The New World sounds its horn to all its evangelists, antagonists and enthusiasts, in bold claim of the English language and all its endeavors. There are those who will rise up. This new renaissance of post-modern verse varies in its expense from page to page, and yet, no expense is spared. The jewels of the world vary greatly, but few are as rare a find as this trilogy of works of the Black Saint: Isaacson at best, singular compatriot of Dymer at worst.

The ulterior meaning does not escape us. She sings, she spins, she sews, and as a midwife, she gives birth: the concepts of God as mother are unanimous. The verse and poet, unbound, do acknowledge a feminine deity and one that is comfort and near. There is a deeper meaning to every line: the chance to sing in body, to imitate the old covenant with verse and song, the rhyme of a desert journey, the shining sonnet of a well-traveled ear—all these compose Isaacson.

The Emily Isaacson Institute
September 19, 2015

Introduction

When I began my journey to find the poet—the person who would write this collection—the adventure seemed daunting. In composing this book, I came across a vast amount of poetry in my soul that was uncharted, an old garden that was overrun by thistles and thorns, as is the mind without the spiritual essence. Somewhere in my heart, I decided it just needed weeding.

Mindful of our origin and our source, we gaze on the vast world of literature as a compass. We see in our godlessness a scratched and imperfect text; but what holds true in the infinity of the human soul resounds from one century into next. Each generation repeats itself, not as its wine grows sweeter.

After every word, likening a computer to a pen, and a pen to a quill, there is a silence. In reflection, the author must pause and contemplate if—as to every diamond—there is a clarity, a truce with time, a moment of hard and bright steadfastness. The game and the craft with words continue—it is rare to find a gem. However, the author of a story not his own will tell it with rare precision, knowledge and skill so as to give it voice.

To shoulder the burden of charity is selective, but to be dependent on it is a staple for the poet to have the time, space, and energy needed to further their task. Dependent on charity once, and earning only a living as a songwriter, I set about the chore of writing to make a space in my human soul for pre-doctrinal fantasy, what sets the stage for a huge amount of fictional and non-fictional work.

The trampled poet, one whose works become ill-used or his time wasted, whose words are uncherished or his pen idle, is in the midst of an enchantment, somewhat like euphoria. The poverty of spirit necessary to write a work of fiction, of art—that will not weight the mind down with further cares but be a source of inspiration—will doubtless find itself in the impoverished sentiment, where words grow dim, lack meaning or seem futile. The poverty, the need to write, the study of language, and the use of a pseudonym all lent itself to this book: in the light of the capture of pigment and tone, the shadowlands of Lewis and Pitter... two poets emeritus at Oxford, writing as if to have dream.

Author of 17 volumes of war-time poetry, Ruth Pitter undoubtedly contributed most of her genius to the inspiration and furthering of C.S. Lewis's poetic talent with unceasing furor—a wave, unrelentless, upon his shore. He was never trumpeted as a hugely successful poet, but was known for his later works. Yet we must write after his example.

The enemy of the poet is superfluous generosity. The selfishness of a task is to create a reclusive hideaway for others to commit daunting enterprises. The poetic world, Victoriana, in this book is one where a heroine is feminine—kind, strong, and epic. The hero is one to suffer both with and without reason. The pursuit of poetry is resident in each of the characters therein.

Whose burning flings supernal things
Like spindrift from his stormy crown;
He throws and shakes in rosy flakes
Intelligible virtues down,

And landing there, the candent air
A transformation on them brings,
Makes each a god of speech with rod
Enwreathed and sandals fledged with wings.
    —*C. S. Lewis*

A kind of transcendence and round-about logic seems a staple to
Victorian culture, which accrues an interesting mixture in *Hourglass*,
with the United Kingdom symbolism, and superstition combined
with heritage. The dependence of humanity on natural medicine as a
structure for early medicine, lends itself to mythology and healing in
regards to the use of tea, herbs, essential oils, and Bach flower
remedies (discovered later by Dr. Edward Bach). Victoria, though
rich in many ways, must let us experience our own poverty first, and
from the place of poverty, move to our dependence on a natural earth.

This earth, untouched, this wild Madonna, furthering birth and
poetry, is handed down from naturopath to naturopath in the interest
of leaving the earth as one found it, first doing no harm, and mother
as creator: the feminine image being dominant as medicinal, kind,
and strong—a mythological medicine.

Shadowed with Jamshid's grief and glory as with eagles' wings,
Its foot-hills dewy-forested with the amours of kings,
Clashing with rhymes that rush like snow-fed cataracts
  blue and cold;
And the king commanded to be given him an elephant's
  burden of gold.

  —*The Prodigality of Firdausi, C.S. Lewis*

The trading of one's soul for fine pursuits produces displeasure, disharmony and injustice; the relinquishment of dilemma for peace, the acceptance of poverty and the honour of it, far above nations, is in acceptance of one's crown.

Emily Isaacson

Isaacson's Hourglass

Dear sister, I was human not divine,
The angel left me woman as before,
And when, like flame beneath my heart, I bore
The Son, I was the vestal and the shrine.

My arms held heaven at my breast—not wine
But milk made blood, in which no mothering doubt
Prefigured patterns of the pouring out,
O Lamb! To stain the world incarnadine.

Sheldon Vanauken

Fashion our bodies from the earth,
and when we are gone we will return to it.

Anoint me with oil when I am born and when I die,
that I may count my days.

⇒ ⋙●⋙ ⟵

Hourglass

The minute grain of sand
through the hourglass, counts
each moment of me,
each person I become,
with airs or plain common sense—
You dressed me in linen,
as the wild grass burrs,
and anointed me with fine perfume
from the paisley flowers of the field;
streaming down my forehead
was your oil.

So I was cleansed from within,
so I walked free like a man
released from a prison.
The temple's gate welcomed me,
the church house sang my arias,
they trellised the treble
and reverberated the bass,
note by note.

The hourglass sand is
whiter than snow,
never runs sour,
is as multicoloured as fire,
and salty as the sea,
pouring and pouring
until it turns again.

Love Poem of the Lily

The difficulties of life cannot overcome thee,
for thou art my constant and divine.
The gilded lily speaks from a royal age,
apportioning regal kindness
as a pillar of society, while youth rage.
Here you stood on a cliff with
the wind in your hair,
you were more savage than mild,
more gilded than wild—
the wind howled,
and there was a long space.

The empire of kindness grew.
Black note. Entwined.
Grace note. Elegy. Rest.
Then everyone looked at you
and saw you were unequally yoked.
The planets and moons began to fall out of space,
and you were out of sorts,
bought a glitzy ball gown, curled your hair, twirled
as a Dowager before the waltz.

Butterfly Tears

I once said I love you
and that love remains;
constant through years,
the blood in my veins.

I never will leave you,
be I poor or of wealth,
as the sun crosses the sky,
without guile, without stealth.

And though the ashes remain of our years,
they are sacred because of our butterfly tears.

Threnody of the Thistle

The national flower of Scotland has its place
in the canon of literature.

Thistle manor, away off the moor,
here the thistle down blows...
and away lullaby, mother sing,
lullaby to a prince and a king.
Here there is no sense of repeat,
just a mild prickly pod bed,
enumerating the signs
of harvest to summer's end.
The trees and the heather
all lean like the wind.

Eventually the thistle down speaks—
down, down, thistle moor,
dusting o'er the creaking floor
to the stone gorse garden door:
resurgence from poverty to kin,
from ignorance to education,
forgiving liniment
from within, cold without
from the imminent
moor fog, hazing our sight.
From cradle to Yule log,
burn foolish, burn bright!

Canon of Bloom

Find a door to the garden
repository of bushels of peonies
in fiery purple as pardon,
effulgent contrast to the spicy chives,
juicy tomatoes, and spindly green beans,
continuance after the planting of seeds.
Armfuls of yellow daffodils
are a brilliant surprise at Easter.
Tulips riotous red—
each plant's color diffuses
with the morning
and rises with the heat of afternoon.

The poplar down blew
over the back fence of
the schoolyard;
I reached for the knobby trees
as I scratched in my notebook.
Herbs, fruits, and flowers
my mother carefully planted, weeded, and pruned,
with an eye for their immortal powers.
A city could flourish beneath this hand,
with prudence. But cities would be tombs.
All for the petals of a brightened land,
canon of faithful bloom.

Burning Cinders

I listened from out the little window
to see if I could hear your song
in the lane,
and when the familiar whistle sounded,
even my dulcet heart gave way.

There was the song of us
that whistled on the moor
before the seasons began,
when we knew we'd be together
even in a foreign land.

There was the wood
that burned dry in the hearth;
I took a coin from my purse,
and counted the face on it
memorizing the moments your touch
reached out in healing.

There was the building of
something new amid the old,
a search for independence,
a need to voice a referendum.

The old country calls me home.
Its architecture has not yet crumbled.
I wave from my window
and write Scottish poems
to the sonorous bagpipe,
the fire, burning, burning cinders.

Dirge of the Daffodil

Rightly in my grief, I remain, clutching daffodils;
fondly yours, and the author of this dirge.

Whether I roll like the sea,
or drift as the clouds,
I always know you'll come back to me.
Though the earth turn swift,
or my life decay,
I always know you'll
come home some day.

When I stood at the church,
and said my goodbye,
I knew it would not be forever,
there's a place in the sky.

Idyll of the Iris

The nacreous, mother-of-pearl cloud
between sunset and sunrise bid
the clay lie beneath the earth,
not yet formed on a potter's wheel,
illusive, waiting for a cup, a bowl, a vase,
to procure out of its shapeless form.
Yet healing emanates
where lack of dying dwells.

The bonny swan rise o'er the calm
pond swells, and iris stands straight—
a less than mediocre gate—its tear
shaped bud, from heaven descended.
Its brilliant hue, a door by which
we entered.
A woman in her fragile form
became purple iris of the morn.

True Lace of Ireland (found poem)

Kenmare lace, abloom floral, austere,
delicate, and ethereal,
altruistically made from the convent
in the tradition of the Poor Clare's.

Taken in by ardent admirers
of the antique art to preserve bright
legacy of lace by prime pupils
for posterity, using the nuns'

Original nineteenth century
pattern books, handwork and design that
flow, beautiful, each one, framed like art,
commemorative lace in a token.

The lace celebratory circle,
this year, in honor of the 150th
anniversary of Kenmare-fine
stitching, bright-bent, full-circle in time.

A Daffodil In Wales

I gave a daffodil to a homeless person once,
measuring the moment's verse into a laugh—
but he sauntered away, crushing its head
into the cool earth until its yellow disappeared.

I took a photo of the sky, watching its clouds
billow and roll, passing into eternity,
and the great wave of anguish beyond the blue
sculpted my very form into measureless light.

My skirts were the garden flowers,
my hair, the willows over the pond,
my lips were the red roses, climbing,
my neck, the white swans swimming.

I gave a daffodil to the Prince,
that he might rule Wales with a rod of iron,
and he read the verse of its heart,
and promised to love only one.

Elegy of the Royal Rose

There was always a royal rose,
in deep red hue, loyal
to a nation: entwining
as I looked deep into time.
The empire that bore
your name wore
the breastplate
with the coat of arms,
and sacred incense.

I was first to hold you,
in the lighted hour of truth,
and last to see you go,
the glisten of lush red,
the blush of pink,
a momentary trace of snow,
birth pang of departed lands—
life nestled in my open hands,
unrepentant starts,
O Commonwealth of hearts.

Sonnets

Beauty alone has right to live;
Beauty alone can only beauty love,
April doth turn her back on January.

Beauty is perfect,
Beauty wins all.
Beauty alone is lord of all.

The raven only flies by day,
The owl by night alone doth fly,
The swan by day and night alike
    may fly.

Victor Hugo

I will look for you in a poem, knowing that we would meet some day. If I cannot find you there, I will look for you in a sonnet.

The very air we breathe must rhyme, or we would not match our rhyming couplet: not find another who so exactly matches our ambitions and passing notions.

———— ◆◆◆◆◆ ————

Sonnet I

I cannot work but linger in the field,
thus cannot eat, but walk upon the hills,
he is the facet of my trumpet pealed,
his labor drives the water from its fill.
O mortal wound, upon this silent hour;
I cannot slay me, I am overcome,
the thirst be quenched and speaking of its pow'r
in chivalry where only I am won.
He works, he toils, he sweats beneath the sun,
and I will write what nature has begun,
epiphany in me dwells to be sung—
for I am lonely, misfit, barren one.
What of my woeful rights do I procure,
to stand and now demand my life mature?

Sonnet II

The beauty of the night aches in my core,
the lights of cities far away, now parched;
I've riveted my kingdoms, 'tis no chore,
and through the woodlands I have stately marched.
In every landscape that I've travelled by,
I've seen the sought divine touch earthly realm;
when all the other cause would question why,
I've simply stated, God is at the helm.
The hanging of the bell is one now rung,
the golden tree bequeaths the ginger pear,
I've sought to finish what I have begun
and tempered every anxious thought with care.
What reason would I capture with a lens,
when all that in its season could offend.

Sonnet III

Winter's existence, here bow to Renoir,
tarry upon the hills with blanket white,
be the stillness of a new bride's boudoir,
the lingering of dusty snow's quiet,
with abandon I walk the silver's crust,
my dark head, with jeweled tiara, crowned,
carefree to know success in all I must—
bright silk and satin of the stately gowned,
as shoots of green appear to deck with hues
from sun on high, the newborn spring in pink
of every color, scent; and shade of blue—
the light here dances at the meadow's brink.
The kindness of season's love maternal,
and trading for all that is eternal.

Sonnet IV

The dream is in my breast that rankled heart,
dividing soul from mind, I tore the shame
from my colorful dress, I wore the part—
singing at first light, that his holy name
were enough to make you steadfast, hungry
for more of the spirit's tell movement, light
over the wild hills and valleys, lonely
without a God that speaks in darkness, bright
as the stars, sacrifice of silver youth,
I was sitting on the park bench, lithe, soon
watching the day go by as a sun-smooth
dance: rehearsed, choreographed classic tune.
I am never more lovely than afraid,
the hopeful hand of violets in a maid.

Sonnet V

The silver bird that eats the apples, red,
perches on the boughs, sings loud, bright and gay,
I woke and listened to his call from bed—
revived my spirit where my body lay.
Never have I heard such joyous song laud:
the simple worship of a creature, bare
to his redemption heaven would applaud,
and reap the bettering of life with care.
In each new day, the rich scent of the pines,
the forest brook which bubbles, frothy, cold—
attempt to give my soul all that is mine,
and retell in myth all I have been told.
I stretch my hands out from my infirm room
where I knew only bleak estate of doom.

Sonnet VI

The seven swans swam round the navy pond,
all there resting in white apparel, pale
in shadows, ivory as snow beyond
the emerald mountain, and meadow vale
bedecked with every lace flow'r, every hue—
their feathers fluttered lightly and coldly
in falling orange, magenta, sunset new
for one more evening, while the lead boldly
flew up and into the beauty of day
over and becoming night, the darkness
rested on the swans that swam in starkness,
lavishing the ground beneath which I lay
with spray of petals from every nation
wishing me farewell upon my station.

Sonnet VII

The immortal being, watching death come
as each proud white flower browns, falls, and dies.
The light of each soul, therein proudly won
to walk with you, hand in hand without lies
that would obscure the spirit world, longing
for that requisite touch, no man's reason—
the true quest of anyone, belonging
to the source of their power, the season
of love, of purity's wait in a line
of witnesses, choosing to be most yours;
taking you by the hand, a diamond fine
as the mortal dust rings clear from the floors.
In my heart of gold is the burning fire,
lest I should now succumb to bold desire.

Sonnet VIII

Dance onward to the rhythm of my drum,
stand burnished in the bronze sunlight of day,
let the shadows sweep your soul by the way
of the iris and star it has come from;
jump at the chance to move to purplish lore,
as a magician would saw you in half,
as the mane of a horse flies by the staff,
come back from the brink of what made you poor.
Stand, hands above, and hail the royalty
we come to this place assuming to meet,
we wait, standing for hours, shifting our feet—
stare at the voice, it commands loyalty:
lilting as the sunlight on the feathers
of great birds, flying into the weather.

Sonnet IX

Do not in stagnant water flow, but swim
in the river with clear springs—at the brim
of sunlight's last clean sweep of sky, as lone
as the moons of Saturn, hung one by one
in your Creator hands, turn brevity
to song and valor emanates from this:
that the mind is theologically
inclined to do war and battles forthwith.
Take out one's sword, and triumph!—slay the foe
at this last hour, when earth is falling low;
into a field, death's horse now circles round
and ends the rider's life on gravestone mound.
What richness would this world to all direct,
that in its bosom, neither could protect.

Sonnet X

The gardens of the night, now shadowed, still
bequeath the fragrant eve's perfume with eyes
that roam beneath the vast celestial skies
and give the notion of sequestered will.
The covered head that bows before in prayer
speaks the vows of enclosure, chastity:
rays of truth, poverty's posterity
and flowers, closed against the night's cool air.
The fountain of innumerable lights
flickering in colors, indigo, rose,
wet mist dripping off the end of my nose,
the poise of every dancing spirit, bright.
The moments of the sunken garden's verse
allure the crowds so fond of sainted earth.

Sonnet XI

The fine art of wicks, taught by yesteryear:
beeswax, in the fine golden dark honey
that melts in a puddle of riches here,
tasted first when young and without money.
Steeping tea to pour, peppermint gathers—
tasted first without white cream or sugar,
seeing if we love herbs and hot water,
speaking in a dialect of father.
O beeswax, melting hotly in a glass,
we take your lit candle to the dark past,
seeing how we are justified by love
and melting at the sight of heav'n above.
Bewitched by which is evil we succumb,
and needing of the light we come undone.

Sonnet XII

While standing against the dark, I am strong,
vigilant and overt, not succumbing
to fleeting whims of others in the wrong;
blue as the bloom of petals, bright being
translucent with the arm of paradise
at my back, a mighty army, armour
shod, a silver multitude without vice,
moving ever forward, no less vigour
in their bones than the day they first set out
to capture the castle of my heart strings,
and from the music of my soul will shout,
I am no more about the little things—
Virulent as warm honey at midday,
I taste the good of life here while it stay.

Sonnet XIII

The rose immortal lends its faint perfume
to petals, mortal red upon the dawn,
and stirring of my heart, I pluck its bloom
then walk the depths of green-wood and young fawn
scampers deftly to early morning's song,
the dew, collected by each web, hangs silk
as love unrequited steels from the wrong
moments of the day and pearl night time's milk.
There dwelt within my heart, one harp—pristine
the upland music of its gaze divine,
and hour by hour it lent its plucked lament
to all who hear within the soul, repent.
The flow'r forever, sorrowful and just,
reaps bounty in the music as it must.

Sonnet XIV

Sea sanded the shore like a piece of wood
and it became smooth as liquid silver,
loving to the earth and sky, salty, cold—
the end destiny of every river;
and I stood with my back to the forest
watching the sun's last fading purple light,
the once burgeoning moon, rising poorest
from a refugee camp in desert night,
where the fire is the only comfort, red
as a mind contorted by the black fear
of having naught, and the distance now said
to be a symbol of indifference near
death, and refusing to dream the future,
which now takes hands and is stately sutured.

Sonnet XV

The light to bear at my last humble breath,
the goblet of oil, cast out purest gold,
all speak of favor's now placed laurel wreath—
the best reward when I am creased and old.
I shall with folded hands, resting, here pray
for my heart's desire to not be lost when
I am gone, the print words to stop saying
all that was delicate and austere then.
For I am but a savage beast, beauty
in my time that cloaked a sorry pink smile
(that chapstick almost choked with song's glory),
in hunter's boots, and brought the deer from miles.
Ne'er in my lifetime did I leave for good,
I always would return with one proved poem.

Sonnet XVI

The flock of geese landed before nightfall,
the sword of beauty divided night's flight—
the crimson breath of sunset's remnant might
repeated in the pond's caressing tall
shadows growing wide and with the moon's white
arm overhead, a clear, smooth, pensive gloss,
reflection on the water, strung with moss,
was riveting and studied, grey and bright—
the two facets submerging 'neath waters
pure, dark night's last star on the horizon:
echoing each other's fascination
and morbid still dance, where nature gathers.
The pondering of creature's dust to dust,
and speaking of the life to morning's crust.

Sonnet XVII

In every just endeavor, let there be
the peal of every heartbeat's thunder loud,
creed from minds of persuasion's honor cloud,
harbinger of happenstance destiny.
In every long-studied word let there be
nourishment to the veins of auburn earth,
great victory, and discourse to unearth,
a veritable map to cross each sea.
In every precious new dream let there be
a moment where it started as a seed,
germinating from a small sterling bead,
and the dawning moment we could all see.
What started as illusion made its choice
to subdue you as its servant in voice.

Sonnet XVIII

When turns the weather to a fierce grey storm,
we plunge into the cover of the trees,
we reign in all our damp with leaf-light's keys,
we take a liking to our thrift dry form,
and for clothing, branches spar decorum,
while flowers decorate the hair, and bees
dance smitten o'er the green treacherously,
now creatures of the woodland and the morn—
we once wore dress within the looking glass
and talked in shadows of the evening's lace;
the sun-filled hours were traipsing to the dance
in diametric meter of the class,
we spun to charity of solemn face,
and bowed to light, enamoured in this spance.

Sonnet XIX A Rose From Thorns

A bud emerged in snowy steeple-white,
clear as champagne was the high-bred morning,
the night reeled back, deliciously warming
the gossamer threads of a spider's might.
A rose grew in dewy stained-glass temple
from sharp thorns that pierced a Saviour's pure brow,
and the garden was wildness constrained now,
cultivated flow'r to mind the simple.
Our lives were complex without the bouquet,
so we plucked each sweetly stained soul of rose,
and the summer wafted innocent prose,
nuances of physician's tourniquet.
If only love would heal the fevered mind,
but oil from roses soothes the heart in kind.

Sonnet XX

We parted with one last embrace and I
stood alone against the world—one small dove—
earth had abandoned me like a lost love,
then I flew upwards into a red sky.
I landed far away on Railway Trail,
and covered my neck in a small alcove,
beautiful as the sunshine resin rove,
streaming, ever streaming, tempering failed
heart from despair to hope and faith—like rings
I wear to ward off the dark in this time.
My sturdiness is now a gift in rain,
and climbing the ancient mountain I sing,
walking toward the curse of the weather's nine
furious storms, pitted against the grain.

Sonnet XXI Jacob's Ladder

Early in the morn, wee lassie, our sun
belongs only to us, as to new day:
the trees move on the cliffs with the wind, run—
gallop as the livery of thoughts stray.
There's a fair space where we spoke in burnished
freedom to tell the ancient firelight tales,
behold the minds of youth were once furnished
with reason and rhyme, cloaked with silver mail
of the righteous who walk to church to sing.
Now they've forgotten the song of the tree,
hills ache with silence where their hymns would ring
as a bell breaks solitude, mutiny.
Taxed, they will climb until they climb no more;
the Ladder of Jacob fell to the poor.

Sonnet XXII Salty Purse

That one low call of evening, stuttered breath,
arrested my thought and dragged it away:
more than moving rain symphonies in May,
wildflowers for the heads of women, wreathed,
children who would never tire and grow old
playing forever in the dusty street,
golden heads in a field of hard red wheat,
shivering by a heater in the cold,
reciting civil lines of English verse,
then hoping for the conscience's token piece,
but subsisting on the fare of crabmeat,
remnant of the blue ocean's salty purse.
Whatever we may tire of while the poor,
is now the indulgence of those with more.

Sonnet XXIII Vintage Lamp

Observing a vintage lampshade in hand,
questioning the blue shadows and the light
that serenade the infant born in bright
starched fabric crib, the blurry tempest land—
the servant stands, beating the cooling palm.
The sculpture of the lamp's enamelled base,
athlete of all pertaining to the race
toward morning—the resistance's oily balm,
mother of this era, a busy throng
moving on, smoky denouement in form
telling of the path beneath my feet worn
to candles from the lamp of moonlit song.
Grassroots binding of the look from wasteful
to the cry for ancient things more tasteful.

Sonnet XXIV Spikenard Madonna

When you stood in the brightened dawn of youth,
morning sun lit your head to searing flame,
the jewel that was your crown bore your name,
and scepter bent authority to truth.
We were orphans, standing in your courtyard,
no bliss of parenthood to claim our fate,
no blimey kiss of death to stir our hate,
she took a bottle of ancient spikenard.
Madonna bore us, pouring out her oil;
she called us all her child in heart matters,
our minds, in retrospect, once wore tatters.
In gingham aprons we would cook and toil,
in the woods and fields, our hands would quick spy
what nature left, rust berries for the pie.

Sonnet XXV Cherry Trees in Blossom

Where the cherry trees touch dusk in descant—
wine branches blossom effulgent bright white,
all darkness of the time for this full night—
I wander 'neath the fading light, recant.
Seasons of my soul were like a grand home
I sojourned in once, for the staid calling
when all life pauses before the falling.
The invalid was destined to find none
of the aforementioned illness beneath
these eaves of healthy grandeur, sunlight near
the slant of shadows, refracted prism tear
that moved over the house, the sea, the heath.
If I, in fury, could my earth restrain,
I would—a hundred blossoms in my train.

Victorian Roads

The sea awoke at midnight from its sleep,
   And round the pebbly beaches far and wide
   I heard the first wave of the rising tide
   Rush onward with uninterrupted sweep;
A voice out of the silence of the deep,
   A sound mysteriously multiplied
   As of a cataract from the mountain's side,
   Or roar of winds upon a wooded steep.
So comes to us at times from the unknown
   And inaccessible solitudes of being
   The rushing of the sea-tides of the soul;
And inspirations, that we deem our own,
   Are some divine foreshadowing and foreseeing
   Of things beyond our reason or control.

—Henry Longfellow

There is a Victorian road I can always find,
even in a strange land.

Where are the realms of heaven above?
I travel an earthly road alone by their compass and map.

Winding Road

The road, as a ribbon, wound through my hair.

The fury of life
is depicted in its fortes,
unleashed by its powers,
drawn up from within—
while others hesitate
you roar from the desert,
kinetic eyes staring into the sun,
mimetic at an oasis of finery.

The wallpaper climbed like a vine,
and you were its flower;
in iris hues, warm and delicate,
you rebirthed prestige
from within a silver frame,
wore each bud,
and named each child
after you.

Victorian Portrait

At times we hold a paint brush for a self-portrait,
    then are captured by another's face.

The vanity mirror over the bonnet chest
hunted my image, creating a self-portrait,
and choraled my maze of human emotion
into the glassy eyes with fringed lids,
bossy curls, nomadic hairline,
purling mouth, with teeth like
knitting needles,
clickety-clack, purl, purl.

My scarf of faith had the same quality
of seven church services, only more colourful,
with wool singing a hymn
of having once been carded, spun,
and dyed. Now the lamb saw
her practical purpose, in giving
of the fleece that would start white as snow,
then drift into other bright-hued shades.

Willow Tree

The mother lifts her child up to the light.

Beside the path, where
I wandered, there grew
the crocuses, gold and lilac—
early morn had invited them
and not hindered their bud,
they called me mother...
A bloom under
the willow bent with years.

Where the knarled branches
lift us to paradise,
closer to the sun and moon,
high in their ethereal limbs,
I let my child climb—
youthful and questioning
of nature's realms and heaven's glory,
of the rising from decay.

Ginger Lily Needlepoint

Antiques are the haunts of yesteryear.

The solid walnut narrow chest of drawers
contained the treasures of Victorian time:
ginger lily needlepoint spoke
of painstaking measures;
a velvet autograph book,
enamelled with its signatures
of well-wishers and sweethearts, rose
and fell with the swoons of youth.

There lay a pile of faded photographs,
children without smiles,
spinster women in black, and men with top hats.
In velvet, a set of vintage silver teaspoons
and sugar tongs tarnished with neglect,
an antique fan aged, embossed with memories
and pewter swirls; a pocket watch,
precisely stopped at half-past nine.

Star-Watching Rose

Make one's way in the world, from the very childhood
that enclosed you in a place of dreams.

Follow the river's edge
where the wild red rose
and dark horsetail grows,
follow the impulse—
on earth, the mountains of stars
can be watched
on a flat rock that
would destroy all my apathy.

Don't resist the moon-watered rock,
capturing and controlling
my stony unimpressed eyes,
with the inspiration not to run,
but to enclose my spirit, to re-live,
to breathe deeply
from my lungs
into the morning.

1800's Rival

The sun and moon are rivals.

The present life and the afterlife rival each other also.

The creaking burnished door to life
named her Rival—
and every woman who looked on the child
glowered white until their eyes grew dark.
She blew the dandelion in seed,
wishing, wondering, wanting—
the fairer life of the meadow
met with the mountain's shadow.

Hoping for things not to be hoped for—
her 1800's purse was black with gold tassels—
believing in things not to be believed in—
on her velvet dress was the beaded bodice.
Forever gone, holding on—
opaque moon and golden sun rivalling—
present life and afterlife rivalling—
the dream of time gone by.

Entrance of Wild

The discovery of a foreign land is as
discovering the country within you.

While I was waiting for you,
sitting in the entrance,
the halls hushed,
I heard the sound of a bell,
tip-toes clicking on the marble floor,
then you appeared, with lips like satin
and skin bronzed, with slanted eyes.
I stood at salute, while you bowed.

Here was a gift from me to you;
a watering of a stone
from many journeys.
When you saw my grand pianoforte,
your curiosity placed one hand
upon its keys, which sounded the note.
Resonating on, as a noctilucent cloud,
we would transcend.

Door to the Sea

Find the door early in life that will lead you into your future.

Stand in the sand—
meet the vast ocean in your bare feet
where the relentless salt waters the shore
pounding it in forgiving rhythm.
Washing my soul this way
with tide pools left behind,
archiving hermit crabs
in miniature mother-of-pearl spirals.

All that she claimed as sacred in her life,
are as the artefacts for a future art gallery.
As a child, she collects the rocks,
shells and seaweed of the shore for her museum;
sea stars are the lights of Stella Maria.
Later, as a gallery attendant, she leads us on a tour
of the museum of human life, its first conception
through final breath and beyond.

White Chestnut

Free the birds to prophesy; fly like a bird.

The feathery bars of a cage
pronounced order from the chaos of
freedom; call me home
and I'll become a ray
that slips through the stark white bars
and disappears.
The moon rising in a half sliver
was red, and called me freedom.

She rose into the smoke and ash,
between the sun and the moon
as a pheasant would rise
into the white chestnut, golden plumed,
primed to recall
all beauty for mourning
with a sweet voice, lilting trill:
no cage can hold this song.

Little Goose

The night comes softly, and tucks
each little one under the eiderdown.

At last I have found you:
your hand-mirror framing curls,
the bright crinkle dress
shimmered like silk—
one of the gowns of a young princess.
In aqua and lavender
the sun melts over the hills,
dusty with the heat of day—

And then, with the moon's advent
the necklace of beads
is lovingly placed
in an old jewellery box.
Through the window
I can see the wild goose garden
where the pond reflects
the house lights.

Kiss goodnight,
little goose.

Water Star Quilt

The door to inspiration remains open
    as long as we cannot control.

Order the days, of thought, memory,
and nature: reap draughts of fresh inspiration
from the mahogany sideboard,
where the English china abides whitely
in the shallows.
Pour the Yorkshire tea
and remembrance, the water star quilt
of first birth.

Here, rare collections adorn
our minds, while our souls search
for elegant traditional recipes—
jubilee cake, cranberry scones,
and spice cookies.
The apron of authentic
cuisine repeats upon
our memory.

Masquerade

For we must all have reason;
and reason will not leave us limitless.

There is no thief
that traverses the night by darkness;
he cannot find the door
to sell my wares.
My soul is no stale hind of rye,
no lime rind shall grace my table.
For I wear a mask in a masquerade,
and my gilded heart is beckoned

By a brass lantern—
the light that shines,
ever sweeping o'er the sea,
the light that shines on me—
lighthouse biding each ship obedience,
the gulf of night opening its dark mouth.
For we are only one step ahead
of the Filipino street child.

Walnut Nutmeg Glaze

All things need to be cared for, and from birth to death,
we are unprepared for the commitment of upkeep.

There was an inner rhythm,
unlike the seashore on a summer's night,
and it caught me off guard—
I could touch the sand barefoot,
and reach the sky,
but my starched nightgown met my chin
and birth was something
I was unprepared for.

There was a blue plate with a fillet
and walnut nutmeg glaze,
only my silver spoons painted it
instead, dabbling in the acrylic, beguiling
the white empty space. And whenever
something appeared that had not been before,
it pained me to carry it from the outset
to its eventual death and metamorphosis.

Proverbial Awakening

The order of morning was the spring of the earth,
papery with fragrance.

There were paper blossoms
on the spring trees
that lined the boulevard;
a woman pushed a baby in her tram.
An older woman turned her head,
but the moment of criticism had passed,
for babies in trams had been ordained
by Queen Victoria, written meekly.

A pair of sweethearts strolled
hand in hand along the inner harbour
where a horse-drawn carriage passed,
his smile was a grin and her eyes were bright—
the color of sea water
when imbued by light at the horizon.
They were in the city of honeymoons,
flowers, and bees—humming, entwining sweetly.

Vine Chorus

A name is a gift we carry through life,
    unlike a blessing of legacy.

How in singing, we are like thee
blessed Saviour, cherished
as our eternal home.
We follow you, as our shepherd
in the paths of your heart,
wandering no further than your crook
would lead us to drink.

Heaven awaits the children
who long after thee;
the vines entwine your door.
A father's arms are open
to those who seek thee.
Your precious care of us
keeps us in this world.
Allelu, Alleluiah.

Nantucket

The moment of noon, when the sun was high,
    was summer's cherished bounty.

    I sat out on the point on a picnic blanket
    and watched the kites high in the sky,
    swooning, tasting the light;
    children held the long strings whose
    wind dancers fluttered with the currents.
    The seagulls over the shore
    gave a raucous cry of recognition,
    and tried to fly as high as the break of color.

    Two women sat on a bench in Nantucket
    with a thermos of cold tea.
    They were old friends, and had come here often.
    The water and the green
    were a soothing patchwork, lulling the point
    into stupor on the warm afternoon.
    "Let's not forget this," they said,
    their memories catching each other by surprise.

Vervain Pathways

A stream of fine perfume flows from the crystal decanters.

The forest threw back its evergreen shoulders
with a throaty laugh,
and I disappeared into its sun-drenched
shadowy fronds;
the ways of the streams
became the vervain pathways of my heart,
the moss became my blanket,
the ferns, my pillow.

I had left the reason behind
that I needed a brick and mortar home,
a fireplace, and a kettle.
For I was warm, in this missionary zeal,
beneath the branches of religion.
Only summer's day could mend this;
no rain or snow could fall
and drive me back beneath the eaves.

Vale from Wildflowers to Seed

Every woman who has both birthed and buried a child
knows grief from the inside out.

I took a brush,
and stoked the rose gold as a fiery ember,
painted the sweet scented way.
All through each vale,
and ripened meadow,
lithe with the lace of the fields,
I filled my straw hat to the brim
with watercolour wildflowers.

I meandered along in this life,
meaning to tell you how I felt
eventually, while you were
carried at birth,
with a soft downy head
like a seed pod blowing in the wind,
and again over the churchyard.
Your body, now aged, laid down.

Sweet Chestnut Washstand

She poured the water where her mind was deepest.

The solid sweet chestnut washstand
held the porcelain bowl
where she poured the water
and dipped her handkerchief.
The purity of grief
wiped her tears; where
love would not suffice,
there was hard work and wages.

Otherwise,
she would plunge down and down
under the waves
and her hair would surface first,
hemming about, with gold flecks
still in her seams, and sides.
The motherload would ring
in her shallows, and haunt her depths.

Horse of Light

Go to the place that knows you,
as an artist returns to their medium.

Take off for the fields—
let your skirts gather the wildflowers
where the circle of the sun meets the earth
and canters 'round its pasture.
Find that great horse of light
steadied beneath her hand,
a master painter's impressionist
dewy breath into the morning's fog.

She lifted her hand again,
a conjurer of ink and paint,
and the rays became a white stallion
with a mane of gold vermillion.
He appears when the light sears
through the cloud, thoroughbred and proud,
he gallops with the wind,
he stands at last light upon the field.

Beeswax Candle

Indian Summer melted chaos of death
and partings into order, the eventide of life.

One leaf fell across my path:
it was as a first note in a symphony of fire.
I was impressionable.
The trees melded with the cool
into an auburn unlike
the smouldering pit burnings of leaves,
the musty chaos and cries of children,
the soft beeswax candle melting upstairs.

It was eventide, dark was coming swiftly.
No longer afraid of my nightmares,
as mistress of the manor—
through the upstairs window,
I let down my hair from its braid
and the lady's maid combed
my tresses, laid out my dresses,
polished my shoes, and lit the hearth.

Autumn's Fiery Mantle

A sunset is a prophet, each reading a day's triumphs and tragedies,
     stroking them over the canvas of the skies.

    When the day settles,
    and sun begins to part for the night,
    it is you sweetly singing I hear.
    The sun melts in the sky:
    a cloak of many colors from a doting father.
    The meld of the sun's fiery departure,
    spun itself in all colors into Egypt.

    The world, with misgivings,
    painted its darkness after sunset.
    But I was a king of this world,
    and the chalice of my wine
    could incriminate whosoever I desired:
    once a prisoner, now a prophet.
    From my mantle of kindness, parts the
    oil for his head, anointing every past hour.

Garden Parchment

Winter's garden, with its glittering stars, icicles, and frost
became the evening where we gazed into the sky.

Shine, earth, shine
with icy furor
at the evening of my soul,
and the end of my life.
For I have lived many a year,
and now I have turned white
as the winter,
my hair of organza wreathed
with dried papery roses,
wrinkled as a frozen parchment
beneath the snow.

The last frost I saw
kept the colour of a leaf burgundy,
and iced it like a cake ready for the tea,
the sky was dark and tumultuous
as Earl Grey,
the clouds were my line of teacups,
striped, flowered, and fired pottery,
the falling snow onto my lace doily,
patterned
the chocolate road
with powdered sugar.

Winter Gift

The gift of winter draws out the light—
    away now from the dark!

  The white sun of winter
  spears the sky, as
  traces of frost ice the panes.
  The browned landscape
  covets snow as a sparkling covering,
  as the ponies are covered in the stable.
  The holly and silver
  are interspaced with red
  berries and flickering candles,
  burning the flavour of balsam
  into the wood house.

  Green cedars in a mist of translucence,
  red said Christmas,
  white said purity of a child...
  Hay in a manger, I arrange
  the finishing touches
  on the nativity at the front
  of a long chapel. The choir will sing,
  and children traipse, dressed as angels
  with heavy wings and gold-strand hair,
  through the songs, away now from the dark
  in the tapered wicks of incarnation.

Red Chestnut Tree

The red chestnut speaks of a pathos released into productivity.

What ring of time
gives significance to planetary measures,
spinning reason
as white gold, like a wreath
of natural solidarity and commitment
to eternal realms beneath your branches.
My child and I took hands under the red chestnut tree
then walked along the roadside.

Her heart was a cloistered contemplation,
mine, a despairing tear, welling
up from pathos.
Could I really worry anymore
that I would not find my way
along this mercy road?
The sweet peas waved
their bonneted heads.

Spring Door

The new day will always be the awakening of new thought.

Here, I dwelt on earth, but heaven was imminent.
The road continued as an amber
wake of cobblestones
through villages of lace.
A flow'r of morn
entwined through the lattice,
I smelt the light,
I felt the warmth.

As a young girl from
her white fresh pillow,
I arose from the ground.
It was the Lavender spray
I diffused into the room
as an activist of women's rights.
When women had the right to vote,
I would sleep late.

Salmonberry Ore

A man must find his destiny in life, even follow his dreams.

I stand in the dust
before sunset.
I am caked with sweat,
beaded with light,
and the valley's eerie parting sight
has illumined and left me alone.
My palms are lined
with doing good, without reward.

But I have no recourse if I fail.
It is just me,
a man against the savage elements,
the north.
Metal is my most desired gift,
and most frightening ore,
shaking scarlet gold
as a salmonberry in my pan.

Harbour

Each ship at sea has a personality all its own.

The sea swept along
the harbour wall,
an immense gray symphony
conducted by the hand of grace
and pattering of feet along
the sand; shore
buffeted its rage with salty fury
pounding sanguine spray.

I was self-controlled
as a harbour wall,
doted on by ships,
dotted with translucent sails,
their handkerchief-white vessels
dabbing salty tears in the blooming
undersea garden. Toward austere
foreign journeys.

Seamstress

Resolve to endure until the reward comes for your labours.

I was the seamstress
of Clayburn village,
sewing in serenity
from morning, deep into the night.
I made my living,
never you mind,
but I made it with every stitch
that continued by candlelight.

Not one to be discouraged,
I was never more alive than when
the wedding dress of early love
was embroidered with symbol
and hemmed to perfection.
It was the groom who rose
with the morning and
lit the sky over the roses.

Raspberry Cordial

The bravery required to rise, and that all may have the opportunity,
is something of the New World.

The new cordial: a summer berry wine,
pristine and clairvoyant,
buoyant and effervescent with a zany tang.
She hit the floor running,
bracing her heels to ice dance—
warming her audience to heartfelt applause.
Her tea was velvet,
her dress, black sequins.

The icing of life was a fairy tale ending
to the beginning of tulle and magic wands;
only a raspberry cake would suffice for this party,
with a carefully plucked cordial rose.
She sat on the mahogany chaise,
never wavered in confidence for the crown
of silver cloud linings and imperfect landings,
over demi tasse discussing triple axels.

Art Stacked Against These Walls

Increase faith in our process over fear of our failure.

Of all starving artists,
I was most content to be
poor, to own nothing in this world,
save the art stacked against the walls,
the life-sized paintings of Bohemian women.
My artist's loft held uncertain
ruminations of pen and page,
the scripts of playwright, actor, and director.

I watched the luminaries
parade by with their advice
beneath my window; they were promising
and exacted their arts and sciences
as a woman compels her child
to perform with finesse, with
a futuristic style that promised
wearing a top hat, a cape, and procuring a rabbit.

Songwriter's Sky

Songstress come out into the open; piece together the scars.

Nature was my living room,
sky was my glass window,
she breathed in and out
with the cloudy wind.
The firs rustled a melody line—
spruce needles, my harmony bed,
the stream, my rhythmic water faucet.
The company tilted the mist
over the cedar trees
and they were cut down, sawed,
and turned into sheet music.

A man stood watch
over the valley;
his childhood was pieced
together in scars,
his only obedience to order was
to ride on without worldly goods
until the song—
"I am not without pain,
I am not afraid of pain,"
resounded over the falls.
"I've got your heart in my back pocket," said sky.

Forgotten Raspberry

Gleaning what is left of the harvest is an old art to the poor.

Really, more should come
from me—more time on my hands—
to pick the raspberries swelling
under the beech trees
into ripe blisters of nourishment.
The juice runs down
my son's face. He is only five, but already
he knows a ripe raspberry is his favourite.

He passed by the row of canes,
icy and silent in the winter once.
He stretched his small hand,
and saw one small left-over berry,
petrified by frost. Scavenged by a tiny palm,
with the hope that there would be raspberries now,
or a drop of blood would fall to the snow
and turn into a forgotten raspberry.

The Puppeteer

The clock ticked at three when two women
    entered the room, one dark, one fair.

Take your brush, put aside Gaudi—
the cupboard swung open to the artist's palette.
Scurry across the page in shades of sage,
obliquely color the moon,
temper the threads of the puppets,
dancing their rage this way and that,
cajole the rhythm of life into color and paint,
acrylic, paper nubs—or puppet's snubs.

The dark-haired woman sat in the waiting room,
in a large red dress with leather shoes;
as she sang and smiled to herself,
I asked her what she did.
"I am a puppeteer," she said.
Then at last a door opened,
and a nurse called for her
to take her injection in the next room.

Diamond Door

There is a multifaceted existence that allows us to believe
more than one thing at a time.

There is a Victorian door of thought
you must pass through,
to decorate the lofty ornate rooms,
and arrange the blooms
from floor to ceiling
with inspiration,
wafts of cedar and balsam rise limitless;
now, hang the snowflakes a child made
to the ceiling by a theocratic thread,
and watch the genius stroke of wide brush,
as snowflakes fall like milky fairies from the sky.

Is the galaxy a mineral,
a plant, or an animal?
Atheists believe it to be a metal,
Buddhists believe it to be a plant,
while Christians believe it to be a person.
The moment earth was visible,
was the moment at which the person said:
"Let there be light," and the diamonds
(each facet said "light!")
appeared beneath the earth's stones
and caves to symbolize covenant.

Come June

An early poem, inspired by Victoria Magazine.

Come June,
I'll find my place
in the sun—
weathered wicker swing
caressing wearied limbs
with evensong,
under the blossoms and
promises of summer:
sweet lemonade
wreathed with mint
gracing my tongue,
and laughter
silvering the breeze.

Aspen Game

The essence of courage aids against foreboding,
guiding our subconscious.

With foreboding, they played "Farmer in the Dell."
A sensible child, she stood in the middle.
The five year old girl with an active imagination
continued the song long after it had stopped.
Intuitively, she knew more about rhymes
than the average person,
and could predict when they would sing again.
On warm afternoons, someone would become the cheese.

She had an inspiration to interpret
their varied meanings, the occasional slights,
the looks, and the sing-song
"roses are red, violets are blue."
She knew no fear. Her deep-rooted
sense that all are safe filled her
with optimism—the aspens shook in the wind,
gazing into the iris of her existence and fate.

Gold and Innocents

The most powerful force in the world is deception.

There was a golden
aura around the earth,
a pure carat wealth,
the mother of all metals.
She hid her deposits of ore in stone,
and the river wound away,
carrying glittering waters
from its motherload.

At that time, the earth was innocent
and pure: only a garden between two lovers.
But evil entwined itself between them,
as a serpent bent on deception.
Lust for gold would grow in men's hearts,
and they would drive their oxen,
lighting fires under them, to press them
on through the treacherous pass.

Promène

An early poem, inspired by Victoria Magazine.

September's verdant view:
light translucent through the
still green and
sun-fire-lit leaves;
country paths followed
in search of my wildflower wish,
out of sun-playful days
into the cool.

Fruit swells sweet,
where mellowed heat
now tends to summer's garden,
and apple-smooth tendrils of
bottle-green vine
climb to shadow...
Out of my window,
I watch the skylarks dive
and feed on ruby stead.

In fields,
we climb the slopes
of black-eyed susans
and render back
those oft-loved autumn days,
where song of summer's heart
still lingers.

Steeping Tea

Early on, the oils poured themselves from the
heart of the Divine Mother into the prophet.

The fauna of the Divine Mother
was a rising neckline of moons;
the soft starlit road, a pearl necklace.
The prophet followed each jade beaded
glimmer of her woodland broach—
the river ran blue in her veins,
a well of tested alkalinity
was the depth of her well arranged soul.

It was the wood and the mother who taught her
to gather the edible plants, to live outdoors;
salmonberries and nettle, comfrey and cedar,
simmer-sear the herbs, boiling,
the deep throated growl of the wilds untamed—
but the mother was always near,
dimmer-dear the call of the steep forest paths,
infusing mint to oils over the fire in a glass bath.

Holly and Hawthorn

An early poem, inspired by Victoria Magazine.

In this season,
wreathed with garland and velvet,
listen...

To the hushed falling
of Christmas stars in the dark,
dusting the mistletoe
with icy silver;
be rich and warm in the
firelight and evergreen:
crimson, emerald, and gold,
radiant in the arabesque of time.

Be joyous, shining,
as the childlike voices of starry carol
walk
whispering
into the morning...

O Immanuel,
O Immanuel, come.

Arbour

When love for life is a flight from reality,
then promote honesty and natural behaviour.

With the illusion of a happy make-believe world,
and a blooming wood to replace conflicts,
the mask of the carefree covered the boy's eyes,
the arbour of clematis flourished, as a miscast actor.
His deep fear of tin artificiality
and hidden inner discord
kept him in essence seeking glycerine cedar soap
and chocolate-covered almonds in a gift box.

With both a pronounced sensitivity
and a strong need to be happy—
in the most natural way possible,
the boy defused problems by accepting
them as part of life and making the best of them.
Critical situations float harmlessly past him now,
while each song he sings bolsters the spirits of others,
nonchalant in the face of the repression.

From Castle and Cottage

An early poem, inspired by Victoria Magazine.

In the mist of snow
at midwinter,
Christmas-red running
down the candles,
stars white and breathless
at the sparkle of lights
on snow
and icy silver.

Pontresina
rosy lilts,
bright-clothed
in the embroidered flowers
of tradition,
light and warmth
to the pealing alpine valley.

Where the true color
of a thousand years
scratched, lingers,
children joyous singing
we chase the winter away
and coals
are the brightest, sweetest light.

Allelu...
March the streets, ringing.

On the Wings of a Falcon

What we hunt for is what we desire most.

The lords went hunting
early on the wings of a falcon.
There were the whinnies
of the two chestnut horses,
then the bays of the hounds.
The hunting horn sounded.
The sun went dark behind a cloud.
They plunged into the wood.

Following the old trail,
the two hares disappeared
and the dogs circled disappointed;
but later, as they approached the pond,
there was the view beneath them,
and they avidly became hunters
of both memories and laughter,
of the best of times and the worst of times.

For nothing is fixed, forever and forever and forever, it is not fixed;
the earth is always shifting, the light is always changing,
the sea does not cease to grind down rock.
Generations do not cease to be born,
and we are responsible to them because
we are the only witnesses they have.
The sea rises, the light fails, lovers cling to each other,
and children cling to us.
The moment we cease to hold each other,
the moment we break faith with one another,
the sea engulfs us and the light goes out.

- -James Baldwin